HOW TO TURN ORDER TAKERS INTO RAINMAKERS

Professional Services
Business Development
for normal people *

** educated professionals
who want to ...*

*Grow their practice
Stop being invisible
Make more money*

I

Charlie Moon, LLC
1410 Hickory Stick Circle
Wichita, KS 67230
getcharliemoon.com

First Edition 2021
ISBN 978-0-578-92476-2

This is dedicated to my wife Mary, who has been dedicated to me for many years. And to Ben, our son, who thankfully is as serious, focused and logical as his mother. I am always proud I get to be his dad.

Thank you to all those who have provided me opportunities. At the top of that long list are:

- Frank Kellert, the guy that introduced me to "before hello."
- Monte Cook, who is responsible for my first bank contract.
- Rob Bolesta, who put me in the car for an amazing ride.
- Jim Shinn, my strongest ally for 30+ years.

I pray someday to be what they see in me.

For a laser-sharp focus on your firm's business development initiative, complete the Business Development Checkup.

Gain insight into your People, Plan, and Process.

Learn more at getcharliemoon.com

A NOTE FROM CHARLIE MOON

I have been where you are.

Challenged to turn skeptical "order takers" into "rainmakers."

When you are telling a professional to leave their office and go talk to strangers, there is a high probability you both will fail.

In 1991, I began working with skilled technicians who needed to leave the comfort of their office and talk to strangers. I have developed a process that works.

This book and my process are not developed by a "good ol' boy who sold a lot." There is no "sales fluff" here.

The components you'll read about help the doubting skeptics e.m.b.r.A.C.e. business development. You'll read about the 7-Layer process that provides a roadmap for success for people who never expected someone to say to them, "Go sell!"
Whether you are alone, or you manage a large staff, there are answers here that will help e.m.b.r.A.C.e. business development.

As you look through this book, when something pops out that you'd like more information about, please ask. Contact me. I'd like to help.

Nothing happens until we say hello.

charlie@getcharliemoon.com
getcharliemoon.com

CONTENTS

INTRODUCTION: YOUR WORST HELL

Regret of neglected opportunity is the
worst hell that a living soul can inhabit.
— Rafael Sabatini

T here was a time when the technical skills of your craft would suffice. Last week a dentist told me, "All we learned about business development in dental school was to hang a sign. People will see it. Your practice will grow."

Growing a professional services firm doesn't work that way anymore. On Friday in the local business newspaper, I saw a small-town bank is moving into the market. They'll be looking for loans and deposits. The same week, a mid-sized bank announced their new director of commercial lending. He needs to validate their hiring decision. His group also will be looking for loans and deposits.

If you are a banker, there are too many banks. If you are an accountant, there are too many accounting firms. It doesn't matter what sector you are in, the market is crowded with increased competition. Small-town firms are expanding into the larger markets.

nto the smaller markets. There is com-
e firms.

and more than a few years, you have
tition. A managing partner at "Jones"
s owner at "James." Overnight, the mar-
and confusing.

little smaller. "Jones" wants to eat and
"James" wants to eat.

Plus, the person who transitioned to James is feeling pain in his stomach because the slice of pie at James contains different ingredients than the pie at Jones.

Let's fast forward to your retirement party. Your worst hell will be if someone clicks on a link to show a video of your career and, instead of showing the "what happened" video, they show the "what could have happened" video. That video, your worst hell, will show the times you couldn't decide. The times you started and stopped. The times you "tried" (more on that later).

There'll be the scenes where your ego ate your brain. It'll be painful to watch the part when someone was there to help and you ignored them. This may be one of those times.

I've asked thousands of people in hundreds of groups, "How many of you went into banking (or whatever fits the group) so you could become a salesperson?" Very seldom do any hands go up. Yet that is exactly what is called for in the new world. Everyone sells.

People who rise to the top of professional services organizations are the ones with the technical skills and business development skills.

If you have had starts and stops, glitches, or problems sustaining a robust business development initiative, you are in the right place.

If you are a solopreneur who is good at your craft but feels invisible, keep reading. Or, if you are not so good at prospecting, conversing with people, or following up, you too are in the right place. Keep reading.

There are two kinds of people ...

There are the kind of people who like to solve their problems. And there are the kind of people who like to talk about their problems. Which kind are you?

If you or your staff would rather work with spreadsheets and numbers, or do anything besides talk to a stranger and "be all salesy," keep reading.

What I will show you is a proven process to disrupt the status quo for business development and sales in professional services organizations. I have developed, implemented and improved this process over a more than 30-year span.

Invest about an hour in this book. You'll learn about the components to get your staff to e.m.b.r.A.C.e. business development and sales. In addition, you will read about the 7-Layer process that produces results in business development specifically designed for professional services.

This process is not a cookie-cutter, one-size-fits-all approach. Parts of it are a universal fit. Some components are tailored to the individual.

When we launch this program, we start "left of hello." Sales are lost before the person says "hello." On this journey, we travel from "hello to infinity and beyond." One of the "you gottas" of developing business is you gotta pour enough in the top of the funnel to get anything to come out the bottom. Visibility Management is a critical component to success. Business development leadership is a critical component to success.

You will learn about these critical components. It's all right here.

"We aggressively wait for the phone to ring."

Talking with Pete at a charity event he said, "We need to go to lunch."

It wasn't long after we sat down at lunch that Pete said the line that sums up many professional services organizations:

"At our firm, we aggressively wait for the phone to ring."

He recognized that the staff, waiting for the phone to ring, would not grow the firm at the pace expected by the people up the food chain in his organization.

Pete is the rainmaker for his local office. He is extraordinarily successful. The voice of experience. The person you want on a prospect call. Highest integrity. Well known in the community. Pete appeared to have it all.

Not everyone is like Pete. Pete wanted more. And the "more" that he wanted was not for him.

It was for the people who are climbing the career ladder at his organization. They are smart, credentialed and technically competent. What they lacked was ability to get out of the office. They needed a process to turn skeptical prospects into current clients.

The staff liked looking at spreadsheets more than looking at prospects. Over the years in professional services firms, many have thought being a "professional" and relying on technical skills was enough. Some still do. They are wrong.

If you would like to increase revenue, and decrease anxiety and frustration, keep reading. This process can change your life.

You may already have a business development program in place. There are processes covered in this book that will supplement what you are already doing and improve your results.

By implementing these processes, perhaps the video at your retirement party will be of your successes. This process develops rainmakers. Will everyone become a rainmaker who converts all the prospects to anchor clients? No. But, everyone will improve and you'll see them connecting the dots, and life will be better.

Focus forward and be like Pete.

> *Pete's story is real. His name is not. You'll never know his real name. We have an agreement. I am his secret weapon. His competitive advantage. At the corporate level of his organization there is a training and development department. And an external sales consultant. Pete uses me. It makes me smile.*

Who is Charlie Moon?

Education was important in my childhood home. "Invest in yourself because that's something you'll always have," I heard growing up. I also heard "readers are leaders," and "go volunteer at the library."

After college, a path in sales and sales management led to what was then called "American Society for Training & Development." I was thrilled. Training and development was my life's calling. I even met my wife at a Trainer Certification program.

For more than 30 years, I have been "turning professionals into salespeople" by providing them with a program that lets them be who they are, and helps them do what needs to be done.

In 1993, about half way through a consulting project for Union National Bank in Wichita, Kansas, I was offered a job. I politely explained that I knew nothing about banking.

"That's good," I was told. "We have plenty of bankers. We need to learn what you know. You don't need to learn what we know."

Here's what Jim Shinn, a retired Executive Vice President of Central Bancompany ($12B) out of Jefferson City, Missouri, said about the day we met:

I first met Charlie Moon when we were both presenting at the Commerce Bancshares Executive Management Conference in St. Louis. Charlie was a Vice President in the Retail Banking Division of Commerce Bank, Wichita. I was Corporate Retail Sales Manager for Commerce Bancshares based in St Louis. That was 30 years ago.

I still haven't forgotten the panic I felt that day. As I sat there listening to Charlie's presentation, I said to myself, "And I have to follow this guy with my presentation?"

His (Charlie's) presentation on his process of sales training was brilliant. He had all the executives in the room listening intently to every word. When he finished, I thought I must somehow get Charlie Moon to be the sales trainer for the entire company. That happened very quickly after his presentation to that group of executives.

Over the next several years, Charlie and I traveled to all the Commerce Bank locations in three states. His training to all the branch managers, retail sales bankers, tellers, local sales managers and other lines of business paid huge dividends. He contributed to a very impressive growth to the company. "

In my entire banking career there are some bankers who stand out as exceptional performers.

Charlie Moon is one of those.

> Jim Shinn
> Retired Executive Vice President
> Director of Retail Banking
> Central Bancompany, Inc.

Since that day I have added tools to my toolbox. I sharpen the saw every day. That could be why Lyman, a media entrepreneur client, said, "Charlie is the most observant person I've ever met."

1. NEW WORLD, OLD ACTIVITIES: MASTERING THE TRANSITION CURVE

In times of change, learners inherit the earth; while the learned find themselves beautifully equipped to deal with a world that no longer exists.
— Eric Hoffer

Start where you are

To thrive in the new world, we need new activities. Henry Ford said, "If I had asked people what they wanted, they would have said, 'faster horses.'"

Ford transitioned successfully to the new world.

The results you achieve will be better and happen sooner if you first prepare yourself and the staff for the transition that will occur. As movement from the "old" to the "new" begins, the status quo is disrupted.

From disruption to transition

It had been a long day. I had been in St. Louis helping bankers overcome their reluctance to make prospecting calls. Betty, the sales manager for the Kansas City region, and I were on the same flight back to Kansas City.

As we waited to board the plane, I asked Betty what she was doing for the 178 employees of the bank that was recently acquired. She replied, "Next Tuesday I'm going out and teaching them the products."

I tried again.

"What are you going to do for the em...ploy...ees?"

Betty answered in her big lunchroom voice ...

"Next...Tuesday...I'm...going...out...and...teaching...them...the... products!"

For 178 people, life would change. There would be fear and frustration, they'd be answering the phone differently and learning a new system.

The loan documents would change and the staff would need to reassure customers that everything was great — while they themselves were worried and scared. Teaching them the products is primarily beneficial for the bank.

We began talking about the monster under the bed. I rattled on about how we could help the employees transition to the new bank when their lives changed. Helping them with this transition would give them an "on ramp" to the new beginning. It would be a win for the acquiring bank, the staff and the clients.

My insight came from Bill Bridges. He wrote a book called *"Transitions: Making Sense of Life's Changes."* Bridges' work was published in 1979. It has been named one of the 50 most important self-help books of all times. The model below is a graphic representation of "transition."

After our conversation, we boarded the plane and flew to Kansas City. I found my car and drove the three hours back home to Wichita, Kansas.

Early the next morning, in my office at the bank, the phone rang. It was John from the Human Resources department at corporate headquarters.

"Hey, what were you talking to Betty about last night?" he asked.

My first thought was, whoops! Maybe I had strayed out of my circle of competence (more about this in Chapter 10) or I was encroaching on someone else's turf.

If I had done something wrong, it was too late to retract it. I'd own up to whatever I'd done and make the best of it.

I talked with John about helping the employees manage transition. And how to quiet the internal noise in their head as they transitioned to the new beginning. Their old reality was gone. The bank that had been sold was a family-owned institution. All customers received first-class service (even the unprofitable customers). The new bank was publicly traded, and customers received the level of service for which their profitability paid.

As we wrapped up, John said, "Interesting. Hmmm … Transition. Is this something you could do for all the banks we've bought and are going to buy?

I was relieved and happy. The outcome of the conversation was a workshop we named "The Monster Under the Bed…. or What to do When Your Bank Gets Bought."

Every workshop started with Bill Bridges' transition model outlining:

- Here's where we are.
- Here's where we are going.
- Here's how we prepare for the journey.

The bank's employees were relieved to discover that their anxiety, doubt and fear are normal. We gave them ways and processes to manage the transition as well as their anxiety.

They felt safe, appreciated and understood on their emotional journey.

The material was the gateway to helping them trust the process, even in turbulent times, as they went from "what was" to "what will be."

While explaining the transition at one of the earliest sessions, a supervisor who was relieved, thankful and scared blurted out, "Where the hell were you a year ago when all this mess started?" Then she smiled. I appreciated her bravery and answered.

Last week, I met with a consultant who was struggling to explain an online commerce function to a client. The client had made progress and then stalled out on moving forward. I drew the transition model and explained what was happening. He said, "This is exactly what's going on. I'll show this to my client."

Working with people in transition is as pertinent today as it was when I first used it over 2,000 workshops ago.

No matter where we are, what we're doing or where we're going, there will always be transition. There will always be the monster under the bed that will chatter like he's on crack.

When the life of a person changes, providing them with the tools to succeed is our duty. Helping them understand and work through the transition is one of the tools.

Life changes when going from a life of looking at spreadsheets to a life of looking at strangers. Prepare for the journey.

What do you want?

It's a simple four-word question I ask often. It's difficult to get an answer. Many times people start the answer with, "What I don't want is …" Whatever is said next indicates the person answering is focusing on the problem. I challenge people to "F.O.T.O." — Focus On The Outcome. What do you want out of the investment you will make by reading this book?

By using the F.O.T.O. approach your answers may be:

- A sustainable business development program through which anyone can be successful.
- For my staff to get out of the office and into the community to develop business.
- The status of creating a well-oiled revenue machine.
- Less worry about where the next client will come from.
- To stop waiting for prospects to call us.
- A process that when followed works.
- To know what to say to prospects after "hello."
- To know how to write a script (but never read it).
- To learn to sell without being rude or intrusive.
- To learn the next steps to move in the right direction.
- A supplement to the current program.

Focus on the outcome. This is a magnetic North Star, a place to shoot for. It's not a goal. Goals are more defined. F.O.T.O.. Trust the process. This is a new world requiring new activities.

2 . PREPARE FOR THE JOURNEY

Have the courage to face the truth.
— *W. Clement Stone*

On my website, getcharliemoon.com there is a Business Development Checkup. The purpose of the checkup is to help you have the courage to face the truth.

The questions are designed around the three areas you must consider, understand and develop to be successful with your business development initiative.

People: Are the right people in the right positions to lead and to deliver this initiative? Do the people have the capacity and the propensity to deliver the results you envision?

Plan: What do you want? Do you know? How clear is the goal? How focused is the plan to get to the goal? Don't arrive in the future and wonder how you got there. Showing up every morning and hoping something happens is not a plan. Yet, this happens in offices and in lives everywhere, every morning.

Process: Having the right people in the right roles and having a plan on what they'll be doing to get you where you want to go is not enough. There must be a process. It must be sustainable. What process is being used? Is it the right process?

When we "F.O.T.O." — Focus On The Outcome — we start with what we want and reverse-engineer the process to where we want to go.

Complete this business development checkup here or on the website getcharliemoon.com to see where you are starting with your people, what is or is not in your plan, and if your process is the correct process.

Total up each number separately. The number of 1s, 2s, 3s, 4s, and 5s.

- Multiply the total number of 1s by 1 _____
- Multiply the total number of 2s by 2 _____
- Multiply the total number of 3s by 3 _____
- Multiply the total number of 4s by 4 _____
- Multiply the total number of 5s by 5 _____
- Add the subtotals together _____
- The last number above gives you the percentage of the current state of business development in your organization.

(See the Business Development Check Up on the following pages.)

Business Development Check Up

A close look at how you e.m.b.r.A.C.e. business development
Rank your efforts on a scale of 1-5 (1 is weak - 5 is strong)

	Statement	Rating				
1	We have a viable sales plan. It is part of our performance metrics and is referred to consistently	1	2	3	4	5
2	We have one person responsible for leading our business development efforts. And-- that person is the right person.	1	2	3	4	5
3	We have a viable sales plan. It is part of our performance metrics and is referred to consistently	1	2	3	4	5
4	Sales plan is visible and used throughout the entire organization	1	2	3	4	5
5	Quantifiable objectives are communicated and support our strategic plan	1	2	3	4	5
6	We have identified and implemented a prospecting "cadence" to keep us "top of mind" with prospects	1	2	3	4	5
7	Key personnel understand, support and initiate business development.	1	2	3	4	5
8	We have clearly identified our target market and our business development efforts are focused on it.	1	2	3	4	5
9	We have a process in place to identify gaps in our sales strategy	1	2	3	4	5
10	All sales meetings are attended by all involved and have a printed agenda. Participants report on progress and when they need assistance.	1	2	3	4	5
11	Our leadership team is trusted, available and committed to helping the organization and everyone succeed in business development.	1	2	3	4	5
12	Our sales goals, including "contact initiation" through "win/lose" are clearly defined and a part of our performance appraisal process.	1	2	3	4	5
13	We have an accountability process in place to manage sales performance.	1	2	3	4	5

Business Development Check Up (page 2)

A close look at how you e.m.b.r.A.C.e. business development
Rank your efforts on a scale of 1-5 (1 is weak - 5 is strong)

	Statement	Rating				
14	We have a sales process in place. It has a name. We have collateral materials to keep the process top of mind with business developers.	1	2	3	4	5
15	Our sales process begins with the identification of prospects and concludes with an "after engagement interview" with clients after a project is completed.	1	2	3	4	5
16	We have referral sources at organizations that help us identify and connect us to opportunities.	1	2	3	4	5
17	We have defined what is and is not working in our sales process.	1	2	3	4	5
18	We study our competitors AND OUR organization to identify vulnerabilities.	1	2	3	4	5
19	We have monthly, quarterly, annual and three-year outcomes and/or goals identified at the company level and the individual level.	1	2	3	4	5
20	We have identified and communicated the impact and importance of business development to organizational growth and individual career growth	1	2	3	4	5

How to interpret your score:

20% to 34%: It's time to address the lack of focus in business development in your firm. Continue to read.You will uncover processes that will change your life.

34% to 49%: This range suggests that the business development area of your firm is "serious, not hopeless." Ignoring a problem will not make it go away. It is time to focus and execute on a business development initiative. Problems don't fix themselves.

50% to 64%: Average focus delivers average results. No one puts in the work to get to the top of an organization only to risk it all by settling for the status quo or being average.

65% to 79%: Indicates you have taken steps to be successful in this area. There are areas of improvement available that, if addressed and implemented, will result in best practices that will supplement and complement your current efforts.

80% to 100%: Congratulations! This score range indicates you have the proper People, Plan and Process in place to prevent problems. Very few companies have the focus and execution process in place to reach this level on their own. On the other hand, your score might indicate Impression Management played a role in your responses.

The computer version of this checkup includes insight into where you win business, where you lose business, and where you would benefit from further conversation, questions and assistance. For a closer view, go to getcharliemoon.com

Companies don't call me to work with them when everything is going well. The work I do places me in situations where there is drama and tension.

As I peel the layers off the onion, the underlying cause of the drama and tension is due to people operating outside their circle of competence. (See Chapter 10).

When life changes

While I was working with a client organization that was full of drama, my brother Tony, a Ph.D. organizational development guy, directed me to the work of Stephen Karpman, MD. Karpman created the Karpman Drama Triangle in the late 1960s. In the 2000s, David Emerald built on the Drama Triangle in his book "The Power of T.E.D." (The Empowerment Dynamic). I became a practitioner of Emerald's material.

Transforming drama into productivity is one of the benefits that happens when we recognize there is emotional turmoil in the workplace, and work to address and resolve it.

"What is" and "what will be" and a rubber band …

As organizations move from "what is" to "what will be," they encounter the "Transition Zone," which was introduced in Chapter 1.

There is an exercise involving a rubber band that is simple yet profound. Go grab a rubber band — or imagine one in your hands — and work through this. Hold the rubber band with both hands. Your left hand represents where your business development program is currently. The "what is" is the current reality.

Your right hand represents where you envision your program moving after taking action and implementing this process. That is "what will be." Stretch the rubber band. As the rubber band begins to stretch and tighten, you are creating dynamic tension. This tension represents the transition zone, the valley of despair, the difference between "what is" and "what will be." When things change, there's always the potential for tension.

There are two ways to relieve the tension:

1. Move the right hand closer to the left hand. The tension is relieved and what you have done is maintain "what is." — the status quo. Unfortunately, you have settled for less than you envisioned.

2. Move the left hand closer to the right hand. The tension is relieved and what you have done is move closer to "what will be."— the outcome and the vision. Congratulations, you are making progress!

One of the two outcomes is happening in your organization right now. If you are settling for less than the optimal results, or maintaining the status quo, you are settling. Reading this book and implementing processes afterwards will move you toward your envisioned reality.

3. SUBJECTIVE OR OBJECTIVE: HIRING SALESPEOPLE WITHOUT GETTING SOLD

"Done is better than perfect."
—Sheryl Sandberg

T he way most business owners hire salespeople is a disaster. Often, the best sale the new hire makes is selling you on them.

Think back on hiring mistakes you have made in the past. The scary and expensive mistakes seem to be etched in our memories. These mistakes happened due to a subjective hiring process.

Mistakes are made from over-reliance on gut instincts. Mistakes are made from taking people at their word. "Trust and verify" is not just a cutesy phrase. Validation and verification are important in the hiring process.

I suggest the verification comes in the form of an assessment. Assessment findings are stories written by the person taking the assessment.

Today, LinkedIn notified me that a contact of mine had changed jobs. Again. I met this person at a networking event nine years ago.

We connected on LinkedIn. I have watched her career path since then.

This person has been hired, trained and trusted to develop business for seven organizations in nine years. That's an average of one new job every 15 months.

Consider the cost of turnover, the loss of business, the expense to hire and train. Consider the damage to this person's self-esteem as one job starts and stops and then another job starts and stops. Proof positive that getting sold when hiring still happens. It's unfortunate for all involved.

Subjective process

Here's what happens and why we make mistakes in hiring people. Interviewing is a subjective process. We ask the questions. The applicants respond with the answers they have rehearsed to cast themselves in the best light possible.

Our goal? Hire someone. Their goal? Get hired. Selling happens.

Not long ago I was talking with a business owner who was struggling. He was hiring salespeople who didn't work out. When I enlightened him on my process for "hiring salespeople without getting sold" his face lit up.

He said, "I get sold. That's exactly what happens. I get sold. I buy what they are selling."

He wanted to fill a position. The candidates were selling themselves in the interview. For some, this is the biggest and best sale they make.

Prior to becoming a user of hiring assessments, a successful manager once told me, "I hired him on Friday and on Monday what showed up was his twin brother from hell."

George Dudley and Shannon Goodson at Behavioral Sciences Research Press developed the assessment I use. They taught me to interpret the findings in 1991. It has never failed me.

The use of the sales call reluctance assessment, available from me, will tell you what to expect when the trainee shows up.

A training and development facilitator with a Ph.D., who has used the assessment for 20+ years in a large bank, said, "This assessment provides a level of accuracy in terms of assessing fears."

Fear transforms into behavior. Behavior is measurable via the assessment.

The person taking the assessment may not recognize they have these underlying fears.

In the interview process, their fears are rarely disclosed or uncovered by the interviewer. The assessment predicts behavior prior to selection.

After the candidate is hired, the assessment then becomes a road map for areas of development to overcome fear.

Before we move on to the particulars of the sales call reluctance assessment, let's deep dive into some generalities about profiles, assessments, surveys, predictive indexes, evaluations, etc. When I started using profiles 40 years ago, I was looking for a predictor of behavior.

Unfortunately, there are nonbelievers in the validity of assessments. That's due to the sheer volume of assessments available. There are good ones and bad ones.

The call reluctance assessment is the only assessment that answers the questions "Will this person initiate contact with prospective clients in sufficient quantities to be successful?" and "Do they manage their visibility?"

The primary question to be answered is "Will this candidate make sales calls or excuses?" In addition, the assessment measures 21 areas of behavior where a candidate may compensate to cover deficiencies.

This profile is the only one I am familiar with that answers the question, "Do we have valid results?"

Three filters measure validity:

- Impression Management — Were answers slanted to create a favorable impression?
- Hedging — Were in-between answers chosen to throw off the profile?
- Response Consistency — How much attention, effort and/or cooperation went into completing the profile?

When working in environments where there is complexity in the solutions provided to clients, it is important to know if the candidate will invest energy into problem-solving. This assessment provides a score for this. Problem-solving is not a measure of intelligence. It is a measure of how much energy and attention will be invested in solving complex problems.

Next we identify the structural dynamics of the individual. How much energy/motivation is available? Do they have goal clarity?

Assessing the amount of motivation (M) a person has will tell us if they have the raw metabolic energy available to get to their goals (G).

The "M & G model," developed by George Dudley and Shannon Goodson, represents the foundational structure of the person taking the assessment. The model below represents motivation and goal levels in sync.

The Motivation score answers three questions:

Amplitude: How much energy do they have?
Velocity: How fast will it move?
Duration: How long will it last?

A "low-motivation imposter" indicates insufficient motivation (M). This is a problem. Observable behavior of a low motivation imposter is someone who is "all talk and no action." They don't have enough energy to support their goals. We wouldn't use a 9-volt battery to start a car. The same principle applies to people.

A "low-goal imposter" indicates insufficient goal-supporting behavior (G). This is a problem. Observable behavior of a low-goal imposter is someone who is "all revved up with no place to go." They don't have goals in place to channel their energy or motivation. Goal setting and clarification remedy this situation.

Goal Diffusion is another imposter. Observable behavior of a "goal-diffused imposter" is someone who "has too many irons in the fire."

Everyone has a finite amount of energy. Goal Diffusion sends energy to several competing goals. Have you ever seen someone start many projects and not finish them? Or do they get distracted easily? Goal Diffusion.

The consequence of Goal Diffusion is devastating to individuals and to organizations. As organizations flatten and more responsibilities are added, Goal Diffusion happens.

Finally, we arrive at the measurement of the behaviors that inhibit the ability to get out of the office.

Using the analogy of connecting an electrical source (M) to a television (G) with a power cord, if we turn on the TV we should get a bright, clear picture.

When sales call reluctance occurs, we divert the energy away from our goal (to make a sales call) into goal-obstructing behavior. An emotional short-circuit occurs.

To continue with the analogy, if we fray the insulation off the cord and let the bare copper wires touch, we would not get a bright, clear picture. Things would not function properly. This is what happens in the mind of a person when it's time to make a sales call. They divert the energy into "coping behavior." It looks like the model below:

The coping behavior manifests in 12 disruptive fears or types of sales call reluctance. They are measured in severity and reported via a green light, a yellow light or a red light.

Green is go — no issue with self-promotion in this area.

Yellow — a cautionary flag, there are bouts of difficulty in this area.

Red — off limits. Unable to prospect due to this coping behavior.

The 12 types of call reluctance or inability to make competencies visible are:

Doomsayer — Worries about worst-case scenarios. Unlikely to take social risk. Limited social interaction.

Over-preparer — Over-invests in being organized, or getting ready to initiate contact. Never quite ready to move forward.

Hyper-pro — Image investment is critical. How they look is more important than what they accomplish. May talk in constrained tones. Needs signs of accomplishment for approval.

Stage Fright — Avoids opportunities to present to large groups.

Role Rejection — Doubts the validity of a career that requires selling, being visible.

Yielder — Doesn't want to be seen as rude, intrusive or pushy. Lacks assertiveness. Overly concerned with being nice.

Social Self-Conscious — Avoids initiating contact with those seen as wealthy, prestigious, powerful, or more educated. Financial services reps would network with tellers, not commercial lenders.

Separationist — Networking through friends is off limits.

Emotionally Unemancipated — Networking through family members is off limits.

Referral Aversion — Does not ask for referrals from clients.

Telephobia — Avoids using the phone to prospect, call clients, or in extreme cases when someone actually does call in. May carry over to social media and email correspondence.

Oppositional Reflex — The only type that can't be fixed. They don't have a problem. Everyone else does. Overly critical. Able to critique everything, even psychological assessments for which they are not trained.

These coping behaviors are measured and severity recorded.

Upon completion of the assessment I interpret the results for the hiring manager. I've had more than one hiring manager tell me, "It's as if you have been following this candidate around."

In addition to predicting behavior in the selection process, it is beneficial and money well spent to provide this assessment as a development tool to the current staff members.

For more than 30 years, I have interpreted the results of the profile and have seen the benefit of helping people identify and correct their self-limiting behaviors.

Prior to the assessment, the behavior controls the person. After completing the recommended course, the behavior is controlled.

Now that she understands the importance of visibility, a success story told me, *"This (profile and training) made me self-aware of all the little nagging thoughts that had been holding me back. Now I hold them back."*

Another person who benefited from the assessment said, "Charlie helped my focus. The assessment he uses identified why I was spinning in circles. My personal and company sales have increased tremendously. More important, he is honest."

Additional information we gather for selection and development looks at "how" a person will act in front of a client. This is a behavioral assessment. Another layer we look at is the candidate's value system. This viewpoint gives us insight into "why" they do what they do.

I had a client who has two of his three grown adult children working in their company. One child made three times more commission than the other child. Dad blamed commitment, closing skills, all the usual contributors. Values were at play. One valued money. One didn't.

People do things for their reasons, not yours. Find out their "why" and speak to their values.

Every strength, when overused, can become a weakness ...

Before tax season, I was working with an accountant who wanted everything to be perfect. Her supervisor said, "It's like she is going to frame her work and hang it on the wall. I'd like her to get the work finished and move on."

Initially, she was nervous about work not being perfectly perfect. Prior to these conversations, she thought perfection was an admirable trait and that she was doing great work.

Over-investing in perfection cast her in an unfavorable light. This approach was seen as a weakness. For both the supervisor and the accountant, it's the value system in play.

There's too much risk involved when making a hiring decision to not use the tools available. Assessments are predictors of behavior. They are objective in their findings.

Use the appropriate tools to get the appropriate answers. Use the right tools to assist in making the right hiring selection.

When you factor in the cost of the hiring staff time, opportunity loss, salary loss, benefit cost and, honestly, just the aggravation and frustration of making a poor hiring decision, the investment made in assessments is minimal.

Investment in the assessment and training for the current staff members at your organization will complement what is currently in place. And will provide a return on the investment. Investment always precedes return. Always.

4 . WHY SALES TRAINING AND COACHING DON'T ALWAYS WORK

What gets measured, gets done. And what gets rewarded gets repeated.

A side from the organizational distraction and management ineptness in running a business development program, there's another reason that sales training doesn't work.

The process being used is wrong.

You've done it or you've seen it. A sales trainer is called in and the training is presented.

After a few weeks your staff is back to spending more time making excuses than making calls on prospective clients.

The reason the training failed is the training started in the wrong place. It started **after** "hello." It needs to start **before** "hello."

There are two phases to the sales process.

Phase 1. Everything that happens before hello.

Phase 2. Everything that happens after hello.

Using the assessment in the last chapter, we now understand the emotional short-circuit that triggers before saying hello. First, we must fix that short circuit. If that is not detected and corrected, you will have problems after the enthusiasm is replaced by disillusion.

Frankly, there is no need to invest in sales training until we know if the people will say hello.

The focus on what is right of hello is due to the denial of the emotional trauma that happens before hello.

Glance over at your bookshelf and see if there are any books that are focused on "what to do before you say hello."

There's only one book that speaks to what happens before a person says hello. There is only one original. Again, George Dudley and Shannon Goodson wrote it. They personally trained me.

In 1991, as a sales manager in media sales, I observed sales call reluctance before I knew it existed. The people I would hire would run out on me when their guarantee ran out on them.

Thankfully, Dudley and Goodson trained me to facilitate their material and interpret the results of the assessment they authored.

The typical "hello to thank you" training is insufficient if you are serious about helping your staff develop sustainable business development skills.

There are hacks that say "just push through it" or "tough it out." These shallow approaches don't work for the long haul. The fear and pain associated with saying hello to a prospect is overridden by the pleasure that could come from the conversation.

Fearful people often focus on the problem. Focus on the solution and approach sales call reluctance with a laser-focused process that is based on research and results.

The quick fix solution of saying "it'll go away" isn't a sustainable solution. The authors uncovered the QWS syndrome. QWS is Quit While Succeeding. QWS happens to veteran producers who, on the surface, look like they are doing alright but are struggling internally.

You won't see QWS on the surface. It grows and develops and production slows. The working lunches become less productive and last longer. It becomes necessary to circle the block ... one ... more ... time before going in to see a prospect.

The phone weighs more. The nights are longer. The prospect list gets shorter. The stomach pain increases. The producer is sidetracked looking for the exit ramp in the transition curve and considers moving to a different firm. They also fantasize about a job that doesn't require initiating contact.

Sales call reluctance is the reason more people fail at sales and business development than any other reason. It doesn't matter how good a person is after they say hello **if** they don't say hello often enough to be successful.

The best producers are the most visible. They are natural self-promoters who make their competency visible.

Think of a famous person. Are they the most technically competent person in the world? Not necessarily. That person is the one who is most visible.

Visibility gets recognition. Recognition gets reward.

1. Are you talented at what you do?
2. Are you motivated to do a good job?
3. Are you goal-directed?
4. Are you earning what you are worth?

If you are not earning what you are worth, your ability to self-promote is holding your career hostage. Lack of visibility and recognition holds organizations back as well.

I have asked the four questions above thousands of times. The common thread is people answer questions 1-3 with an affirmative "YES, we are talented, motivated and goal-directed."

After asking, "Are you earning what you are worth?" the workshop participants get a blank look on their face, the hands that were prepared to shoot up settle in their laps or on the desk. They look around the room avoiding eye contact. They are not earning what they are worth.

In the professional services sector, the workers have done the hard part. They have earned their professional designation. They are not earning what they are worth because they are unable to self-promote and make their competencies visible.

It is not the most technically competent person who is the most successful. Those who make their competencies visible to the most people are the highest paid and most successful.

The No. 1 problem today

The truth of the matter is your people are not saying hello to enough of the right people. They are not saying hello to the right prospects. They are coping with saying hello. They are making excuses, not contact. This is the No. 1 problem in business development today.

Closing skills don't matter if you don't have anyone to close.

Memorizing the exact perfect script doesn't matter if you don't have anyone with whom to share it.

Knowing every detail about every detail doesn't matter if there's no one to tell.

You gotta say hello to more people. Hello is the most important word in the life of a business development person.

If your people are not saying hello to enough people, nothing else matters:

- Not beautiful brochures.
- Not your website design.
- Not a book.
- Not the newest line of trinkets and trash.
- Nothing. Nothing else matters.

There is nothing more important than saying hello to a prospect.

Where did all this coping behavior start? How did people learn to not talk to strangers? Why is it so difficult to say hello?

What created this invisibility issue?

We learned the majority of this coping behavior, this sales call reluctance, this visibility management problem, this invisibility issue from ... are you ready?

From well-intentioned people looking out for our best interests. It was probably learned from Mom and Dad who likely learned it from people of significance in their lives.

"Don't talk to strangers," "stranger danger," "good kids are seen and not heard" ... and all the well-intentioned advice we receive as children carries over into adulthood.

Bankers back in the day sat behind their desks and business owners sat in the beggar chairs and groveled to receive consideration for a loan. Is it really that difficult to understand why some banks struggle with developing an officer-calling program that delivers results?

The other excuse I hear is "good work speaks for itself." It may, but not loud enough for anyone to hear it.

Sales training doesn't work if we only focus on the "hello to thank you" component. We must first get people through the emotional short-circuit so they say hello to enough people to be successful.

How much revenue is lost due to your people not initiating contact with enough prospects? How many careers are held hostage in your organization because your people don't consider the fact that they make excuses rather than calls? I like to say "You can make sales calls or make excuses. You can't do both."

A successful convert to visibility management told me, *"Now that I have conquered my fears around sales call reluctance and making sales calls, my confidence has morphed over into other areas. I recently had a meeting with the managing partner and the CEO of a prospective client. I was comfortable and they were listening to ME."*

The comment above speaks to a side benefit of developing business development skills. Confidence increases and people are more confident to speak up and contribute to meetings.

Why a lot of coaching doesn't work

Coaching doesn't work when it is misdirected into visiting that is not tied to results. The process I have developed, that you'll read about in Chapter 8, will cover the two most important words in a sales leader's vocabulary: accountability and consistency.

Holding people accountable for their business development efforts is the only way to get results. Holding them accountable helps. Holding them consistently accountable works.

When the participants complete their "IDP" (Individual Development Plan), we apply the three tactics to their goals.

- Is there a target?
- Is there a strategy?
- Is there pursuit?

Pursuit of the strategies comes by developing tactics to support the strategy. Plus, if it's someone else's goal it may not get the attention necessary. Ever set a goal for a spouse to lose some weight? How did that work out for you?

Pursuit … execute. We'll cover more about this in the e.m.b.r.A.C.e. model found in Chapter 7.

To measure the progress on the goals that are set, I use accountability metrics. Using software, we enter the metric from the IDP and track progress in meeting the goal. There's no ambiguity.

Did they or didn't they meet their goal? The results are displayed in color. Green indicates goal-supporting behavior. Red indicates goal-obstructing behavior.

When a person being coached gets off to a rocky start and their goal is not met, a red dot appears on the goal timeline. After a couple of red dots appear, they see this is a real thing. Their compliant nature kicks in and the necessary changes are made to the approach.

Behavior changes. Results happen. When the goal is met, a green dot appears. As the person being coached continues to meet the goal, they receive green marks. The goal line starts to fill in with green highlights or red highlights.

Last summer I was working with a CPA. She embraced business development and this process. A professional and well-established in her career. She smiled and told me, "Green is good. Red is bad ... I only want green." The point is progress was made and the goal was met.

Another benefit of using software is the completion reminder. They are implemented to ensure tracking is completed. When the meeting is Tuesday at 10 a.m., we agree that the progress toward the goal needs to be entered by Monday at 5 p.m.

If the numbers are not entered by that deadline, a text or an email is automatically sent to remind the individual to do so. Accountability and consistency work. More about this in Chapter 8.

5 . WHAT MICROWAVE POPCORN AND GARAGE DOOR OPENERS TEACH US

"When we need a friend it's too late to make one."
— Mark Twain

In today's world, we expect immediate results. We put a flat bag of popcorn in the microwave, push the popcorn button and within a few minutes we have a big fluffy bag of popcorn. Results: immediate and easy.

We turn the corner, head toward our garage, push the button and the garage door opens. Results: immediate and easy. When do we expect results? Immediately and easily.

This "immediate and easy" world we have created through technology and connectivity has bled over into everything in our lives. Immediate and easy has become our mantra. If it doesn't happen immediately and easily, there must be something wrong.

There are unintended consequences of this world we have created. We lose our focus if something doesn't happen in an immediate and easy manner.

But business development doesn't happen in an immediate and easy manner.

Building a relationship that moves us from "stranger" to "trusted advisor" may take years — yes years — for a new prospect to become a current client.

There is no silver bullet. It will take dedication and focus for a person who would rather look at spreadsheets to become a person who is comfortable talking to strangers and leave the comfort of their surroundings to go on a business development call.

The longest journey begins with a single step. We must take that first step.

Expecting immediate results from your new business development initiative is like expecting flowers the same day you plant the seedlings you purchased at the big box store. With the greatest intentions, we buy the petunias, take them home, put them in the flower box, and water them diligently. The sun shines, the temperature warms up, and a few weeks later, we proudly announce during dinner, "We have flowers."

We don't plant the seedlings we purchased on Saturday and go outdoors on Sunday and pull them out of the ground to see why they aren't blooming. And then pull them out of the ground again on Monday, and then again on Tuesday and then again on ... well, you see where this is headed.

Developing business is a **process**. We have a process for our process. Let's have a process for changing behavior.

> "Using a process turns grass into milk."

Let's apply a process to changing behavior and getting people out of the office and into the community. Keep in mind we are turning around a barge, not a kayak.

Back to "F.O.T.O." — Focus On The Outcome. What outcome do we want at this point? Do we want results? Or do we want "activity"?

Activity or results?

At this point, we want activity. We want the staff to "do something." We won't get results without activity. Lack of activity is the death knell of business development initiatives in professional services organizations. Start with activity.

Set the bar low. Set the bar low enough so the people you are training find success. Set the bar low enough that you can, as Ken Blanchard told us, "catch them doing something right." They need to win at this point. You need them to win at this point.

A good place to have activity before you have competence is with prospects that don't matter. Or have conversations with people you know are safe. Don't have a "new to the process beginner" call on an "A+" prospect. Start with easy.

I recently worked with an individual who, based on her profile that we talked about in Chapter 3, was "telephobic." She was not going to pick up the phone and call a current client to thank them for their business.

What she could do is build beautiful spreadsheets. She loved building spreadsheets. I could hear a sigh of relief and see her smile when I asked, "Could you build a spreadsheet of your current clients we can call and thank them for their business?" Notice I said, "we can call."

Building a spreadsheet gave her a business development task that she could easily succeed at. And, it gave me the
opportunity to "find something good" that she did, and encourage her.

Plus, we needed a list to call. Next, we wrote a script of bullet points of what she would say when she calls the current client. Always have a script.

A bullet point script keeps them on track while their heartbeat increases, their breathing gets shallow and their stomach hurts.

Always have a script, but never read it.

Scripts keep the caller on track. Scripts keep the prospect on track. It may take all the courage a person has to make a phone call.

I worked with her on what to say first, and why. What to say second, and why. What to say third, and why. We also covered what not to say. And, we covered what to say when the prospect says "send me some information." I believe in the positive power of negative preparation.

I do ... we do ... you do ...

The success mantra I use is "I do ... we do ... you do." When it's activity time and we get to the part that is going to create the least comfort (in this case, picking up the phone and entering the number), I demonstrate the behavior we want.

I do. I called four current clients. I got four voice mailboxes. Then we debriefed what happened.

We do. Now, it's her turn, I reassure her that I am here for help and support. She dialed the number. She left some voicemails. This is activity. Activity builds momentum. Momentum gets results.
The "we do" step is me, encouraging and reassuring the person making the calls that they are doing something right.

You do: After the behavior we want is observed and then mimicked, it's time for the "you do" stage.

A short time later, the person who previously was unable to use the phone offered this up in a session:

> *"I remember the days of going into one of the partner's offices and asking him a client question. He would say, 'Let's call them.' And then he would just pick up the phone and dial the number. Now I am able to do that. I just pick up the phone and call."*

The behavior you get is the behavior you reward. In the beginning, a plan and a process coupled with encouragement and support is the right reward.

Activity builds momentum. Momentum gets results.

Whatever activity you are doing, make sure to end on a good note.

When you end on a good note, the next time you'll start in a better place. Have you ever taken the family on a vacation that ends with a long drive home? Later, when the grandparents ask, "How was your vacation?" the kids moan and say, "All we did was drive."

They've forgotten the fun before the long drive home because the law of recency kicks in.

If what happened last for the people learning the process of business development was not pleasant, or successful … that's what they will remember. They'll remember the bad. You want them to remember the good. End in a good place.

The same reasons that individuals fail at becoming successful in business development are the same reasons organizations fail at implementing a successful business development program. Not having enough activity. Expecting results too soon. Using the wrong process.

When the wrong process is used, the results don't happen and disappointment sets in. People don't like to disappoint or be disappointed, so they avoid what is making them feel disappointed.

You'll see:

- They are too busy.
- They feel overwhelmed with other duties.
- They move business development to the back burner.
- Business development is forgotten.

If you want, we can wait while you think of all the excuses you've heard when business development efforts fail.

Einstein said, "The thinking that got us here won't get us where we want to be." Using an internal resource at your organization will not get you where you want to be. To grow a business development culture, it will be faster and cheaper and more successful to have an external resource implement the BD process.

Putting an internal resource in a leadership position of building a BD program puts an "unconsciously incompetent" person in a position to lead "unconsciously incompetent" people.

Unconsciously incompetent means they "don't know what they don't know." On this particular XY graph, you want to have someone who is "consciously competent," meaning they "know what they know" and are able to lead and develop participants to where they also "know what they know."

Is implementing a business development culture hard? It is for the unconsciously incompetent. Is it difficult? It is if it's outside the circle of competence (Chapter 10). Is it possible to develop a business development culture? Yes!

We are not making popcorn in the microwave and we're not opening the garage door. We are building skills and abilities that will be with people their entire career. Use a process that works. Let's coach and support and develop people. Let's do it right.

When you use the correct process, you will create results.

Trust the process.

6. THE TECHNICIAN'S BLIND SPOT: WHY YOU'LL NEVER SEE IT COMING

*"Every strength, when overused, can become
a weakness."*
— *Bill Bonnstetter*

Deepak Chopra was on the stage. He cited a Harvard study that exposed kitties to an environment that contained only vertical planes. Yes, Dr. Chopra called them kitties. In this study, there were no horizontal planes. When the kitties were put in a room with chairs, they would bump into the horizontal rungs of the chairs.

Since the kitties had not been exposed to horizontal surfaces they didn't know horizontal surfaces existed. This study serves as a metaphor about your staff. It could be about you.

If someone has never seen good, he or she can't describe it. What they describe is what "good" looks like to them. They may be unaware of what good really is and what it looks like.

We don't see things the way they are, we see them as we are, which I think is a loose translation of Shakespeare.

Not always right. Never in doubt

Confidence is good. But when the strength of confidence is over-used, it becomes a weakness.

Right or wrong, it didn't matter. He was always right ... in his mind. He would forge ahead with great conviction. Following this person would not be a great place to be.

Forging ahead on a path where there is a blind spot is both danger-ous and reckless. Asking for help isn't a sign of weakness.

Everyone has unconscious blind spots. The only person who didn't have blind spots was Jesus — and they crucified him.

Working with processes
We had been working together to move a project forward when I uncovered a blind spot in the engineer's makeup. As I coached the engineer on how he could provide the prospect with a solution, he continued to struggle with the validity of the question the pro-spect asked. The engineer sighed and said,

"Things go really well until you get people involved."
The engineer was more comfortable with the processes he under-stood, and would benefit from help in understanding himself and then others. To better understand others first we need to under-stand ourselves, and then others. Behavioral assessments are a good place to start.

I am not indecisive ... am I?
He was a good guy, but he was operating from a position of fear. He had a problem. I was called in. Due diligence was done to uncover the real problem, not just the anxiety around the problem.

I interviewed the critics. A common theme emerged. "He's so in-decisive. He can't make a decision."

Later as the client and I debriefed and reviewed the white paper together, he noticed the "he's indecisive" comment. He sat up straight, on the edge of his chair, firmly banged his desk with his fist and loudly proclaimed, "I am not indecisive!" Within a couple of seconds, he leaned against the back of his chair.

In a quieter, more resigned tone as he questioned himself he said, "Well … I don't think I'm indecisive," and finally he laced his fingers together, put them on top of his head, and leaned back even more. He quietly said, "Well, I don't know. Maybe I am indecisive."

Finally, as he slid into a slumped position, he asked me "Do you think I'm indecisive?"

He was unconscious of how the changes in his work-life environment, his reporting structure and the company ownership had caused his fear to rise. He was blind to seeing that making "perfect" decisions was paralyzing forward movement.

Fortunately, when he pulled up about 10,000 feet, he saw what others were seeing. The transition curve was traversed and the new beginning became his new normal.

Blind spots happen

Today, I had lunch with a client and his prospect. The client told stories that were excellent. He created tension, then relieved that tension and made his company the hero. I was excited. This client is new and struggles with the process of business development. That's his blind spot.. He is a business development person. He just doesn't recognize it yet.

Professional services organizations attract a large amount of high-level, high-quality people. They set high standards for themselves. They put pressure on themselves — and on others to deliver the highest quality service. They try to "out-perfect" themselves.

They set standards so high that others can't reach them. They set their standards so high that they can't reach them. They aim for perfection. They never want to fail. In business
development, they are so diligently avoiding failure that they do

fail. They avoid failure, and that is their failure.

Done is better than perfect
In a virtual meeting, a prospect asked for additional information, which needed to be sent to the prospect immediately. What actually happened was the business developer wanted to send the prospect the "perfect" information with the "perfect" cover letter.

Six weeks later, the information was sent. With no sense of urgency, the prospect had lost interest, and the sales cycle was delayed by six weeks.

Keep an eye on activity, momentum and results. Don't let your staff get caught in the trap of being perfect and getting paralyzed.

Remember ... every strength, when overused, can become a weakness. Keep your eye on the strengths of your staff and help them work through overusing their strengths to their own detriment.

There is no medal or award for the leader who is able to think faster than people can move. Stay with your people.

Truth trumps politically correct
I can see that thought bubble over your head. It says, "If it's a blind spot to me, how do I see it? I'm blind to it." Good question, thank you for asking. Ask an objective third party that you trust for feedback. Ask someone who will be honest with you.

Asking for feedback from someone who reports to you is not the answer. You run the risk of them telling you what you want to hear. They are not lying. They are managing the truth. Plus they don't want to run the risk of telling the boss something that will result in them getting the stink eye. If you trust your spouse or significant other to tell you the truth, ask.

7. E.M.B.R.A.C.E. BUSINESS DEVELOPMENT

"Success in life is how we cope with Plan B."
— Marilu Henner

When life changes, and a skilled technician sees that Plan A no longer provides the career trajectory they envisioned, it is time to move to Plan B.

Plan B in this case is the e.m.b.r.A.C.e. Business Development Process — Education. Mentorship. Birth. Routine. Accountability. Consistency. Execution.

As the transition to e.m.b.r.A.C.e. business development is beginning, people will respond with one of three mindsets:

1. Ignore the new initiative
2. Discredit it
3. Accept it with fear

Acknowledge the three attitudes in your rollout meeting. Follow up by explaining the transition curve. This creates transparency and shows empathy.

Provide an overview of "here's where we are" and "here's where we are going," and then "here's how we are going to get there." Leaders lead.

You will notice in the title that the "A" and the "C" are upper-case. They are the two most important components to creating a sustainable business development or sales culture. They get their own chapters.

E. is for Education

In this component, we provide the learners with an overview of each step of the 7-Layer process. We lay out the success route from "left of hello" all the way through to the "follow-up cadence." The specific vision and objectives of the initiative that are shared will have been identified by the leadership team of the organization. To demonstrate the organization's investment in their success in this initiative, we give insight into the tools to change their team's self-limiting beliefs and equip them to improve and develop their skills.

M. is for Mentorship

Here's what a convert had to say, *"I learned the value of visibility. Since working with Charlie, I have worked on a national conference committee and will present at a national conference this summer. Before, I would have thought someone else is more qualified. Building confidence in bite-sized chunks works."*

B. Is for Birth

There are three steps to birthing the business development initiative in your organization:

Step 1 — Conception. Create a clear path forward. Take action. To paraphrase Andrew Carnegie, "The older I get, the more attention I pay to what people do and the less attention I pay to what people say." Move forward. There is no try. "Trying" to develop a forward-thinking business development culture is just a noisy way of not doing it.

Step 2 — Gestation. This is the part where the Plan and Process are developed, based on the objectives and strategic plan of the organization. Get the vision of the leadership team involved.

Be careful of asking too many people for too much input. Committees get bogged down, can't make decisions and nothing happens.

Step 3 — Birth. Bring life to the Plan and the Process, and equip yourself with the skills to manage the organizational transition when life changes.

In one of the more than 2,000 sessions I have presented, I told the group that it is "easier to give birth than to revive the dead." One of the participants loudly protested and said, "Of course a man would say that." I corrected myself and said, "Giving birth happens a lot more often than reviving the dead."

This birth component is a reminder that some people will not make the transition from the "old" way of doing things to the "new" way of doing things. That's OK. When you have provided them with the opportunity to be successful in the new environment and they don't respond, it is time to "bless and release" them.

You can't want it more for them than they want it for themselves.

R. is for Routine
As the Process is implemented, there will be starts and stops. There will be times when it seems you took one step forward and two steps backwards. There will be people who take the exit ramps in the transition zone.

As in hiring, the use of assessments will predict behavior and identify gaps among existing employees that, until now, were simply speculation based on opinions couched in terms of "I think" or "maybe."

The assessments will clear all the smoke and mirrors out of the room. Finally, you will have a clear view of what you are working with, based on objective reality.

The "new routine" will become "the routine" as time passes and skills develop. Results will happen. "The routine" finally becomes the "new normal." The "new normal" becomes "the normal."

To make this transition as smooth as possible, sharing information with the staff as early as possible will help them prepare for what's coming.

When people believe they are treated fairly and are equipped with the information that allows them to prepare for the changes, they will begin trusting the leadership with the vision and appreciate the consideration.

However, there may be starts and stops. Don't stop. Stay focused on the outcome and committed to your commitment. In the thick of things, you may be tempted to take an exit ramp yourself. Don't. Instead, focus forward.

In Chapter 8, we uncover the two most important words in creating a sustainable business development and sales culture. These two words change lives and organizations. I've seen it.

8. THE TWO MOST IMPORTANT WORDS

"Success doesn't come from what you do occasionally;
it comes from what you do consistently."
— *Marie Forleo*

I t was a mess. In the beginning, it felt like a daycare center not a professional services organization. The inmates were running the asylum. They had hired me over the phone, paid what I asked and added a performance bonus. They wanted their problem fixed. The division leader had been indicted and sent to prison. Some middle managers had six supervisors in the past two years. It was a mess.

Fast Forward: The process had worked, again. Turnover was minimal. Every one of the 150 customer-facing employees had a performance-based pay plan. They were making money. I was making money. Life was fun. And ... the project was fun.

How did this happen? What transformed the mess into the best? The answer can be found in two words. Get a pen and circle them. Write these two words backwards on your forehead so when you look in the mirror you will see them. These are the two most important words in a manager's vocabulary:

Accountability and Consistency

- Hold people accountable for their performance.
- Set the expectation.
- Commit to goals using Individual Development Plans.
- Develop and maintain consistency in coaching sessions.
- Conduct periodic performance appraisals.
- Develop standards of performance.
- No surprises at performance appraisal time.

Hold people accountable for their performance. I'm not advocating puffing up your chest and saying, "I'm the boss, that's why." That doesn't bode well with humans.

Empathy as well as direction, coaching, supporting and delegating is a civilized approach to leadership. Set the expectation and communicate it clearly, focusing on the organization's goal.

Hold people accountable, including you. Do what you say you're going to do. Be strong. Be brave. Stay the course.

Develop the message and implement the vision. Follow through. The word gets out. People align with the vision. Especially when the e.m.b.r.A.C.e. components are in place.

The leverage components include:

- Application to the program.
- Individual Development Plans.
- Internal Accountability Coach.
- External Accountability Coach.
- Accountability Metrics.
- Software tracking.
- Data recording.

Consistency works
Week after week, month after month. Same time. Same chairs. Same room. Hold a group reporting meeting. The purpose of this meeting is twofold. Participants report "what I did last week" and "what I'm doing this week."

Consistency works when the reporting process is in place. It will take about two minutes for each person to report their activity and results.

The "activity" reporting tells us if they are completing the activity that will develop the momentum to achieve the goals in their Individual Development Plan. The "results" reporting let us know their activity in moving a prospect closer to becoming a client.

In the coaching software, the participants track their activity and results. The tracking is a numeric reply to a system-generated email. It literally takes seconds.

The person reporting their results designates the outcome of each call.

There are two primary objectives of a sales call:

advance — or continue.

One example of an advance is when the internal advocate involves their supervisor in a joint meeting and the supervisor says, "Bring us a letter of engagement." This is a successful call.

A "continue" is when the process continues without forward movement toward becoming a client. If the supervisor said, "This is interesting," that is an example of a "continue." This is an unsuccessful call.

As the reports come in, participants benefit from hearing the others' successes. They are able to extract and apply what worked for others that could possibly work for them. The reports of the hits, runs and errors creates camaraderie and a team environment. It creates explicit encouragement and implicit pressure.

When someone is out or on vacation, he or she turns in their "continue/advance" report in advance. It is read in the meeting. Each person has their two minutes of fame in every meeting.

Displaying the accountability metrics in the software on a screen while the activity and results are reported adds an additional layer of accountability.

Tuesday at 10 a.m. is a great time to hold the reporting meetings. When held later in the week, procrastination creeps in, results sag and excuses rise. Avoid Friday because the pending weekend is an interruption to progress.

"Tuesday at 10" gives the team all day Monday and a little time on Tuesday to tie up the previous week's activity and track their results. No excuses.

I'm not a fan of calling people out in front of their peers. Additional coaching is done in private. The development level of the individual determines if they receive direction, coaching, support or delegation.

Two kinds of power

Hold people accountable through two kinds of power: position and personal. Position power is what you have when you're "the boss," when you evaluate performance, an individual's reporting line rolls to you, and you decide when or if a person is promoted.

Position power strengthens the role of internal accountability coach. That person has access to the accountability metrics we set in the Individual Development Plan.

Personal power is what an external accountability coach has. An external person needs the support of internal resources to help hold people accountable. Without the support of position power, I've seen people shrug their shoulders as if to say, "You're not the boss."

For whatever reason, if a participant sabotages their success or, most often, needs support or encouragement, it's beneficial to have position power involved. Leverage works. Each participant has an internal accountability coach. Position power works.

Archimedes, a Greek mathematician born in 287 B.C. said, "Give me a lever long enough and a fulcrum on which to place it and I shall move the world." Leverage works. Having the leverage of an internal accountability coach coupled with an external accountability coach is the perfect combination.

An additional leverage component that is effective is to have the participants apply to be in the program. We tend to take better care of things we earn versus things we are given. Earning a seat in the program creates commitment and leverage.

The application questions are written to ferret out if the applicant is serious about their development or just applying because they think it's expected. The answers to the questions reinforce their "why." The answers also serve as a reminder to the participant, should someone stray or become complacent.

Participation in this program will pay benefits to them throughout their career. We want those who are accepted to appreciate the opportunity and be aware you are making an investment in their future.

Accountability is driven by data from the Individual Development Plan. The accountability metrics are entered into the software, tracked and available to all involved.

This provides quantifiable objectives to monitor progress. Did they meet the goal or not? Internal accountability coaches are busy. They need data to provide guidance. With the coaching software, the information is not only black and white, it is also red and green.

Then, during the coaching session, there's no more "how's it going" conversations where the person being coached says, "OK, how are you?" and then turns into "How 'bout that game?"

"I'm better at keeping promises to others than I am to myself. By using the software, I knew my boss could see my activity and that kept me on track," spoken by a CPA.

Now that you are familiar with the first six components of the e.m.b.r.A.C.e. model, all that is left to do is to add the final step.

Execute the plan and the process to develop the people.

E. is for Execute

Execute doesn't take long to explain. "GO" sums it up. Strategy without execution doesn't work.

9. THE 7-LAYER BUSINESS DEVELOPMENT PROCESS

Using a process turns grass into milk.

With the e.m.b.r.A.C.e. components in place, it is time to add the 7-Layer Business Development Process.

1. F.O.T.O. (Focus On The Outcome)
2. Managing Transition When Life Changes
3. Start Left of Hello
4. From Hello to Infinity and Beyond
5. The Prospecting Cadence
6. The Engagement Cadence
7. The Follow-up Cadence

1. Focus On The Outcome — Decide where you want to go.
The process I have developed over more than 30 years of professional services business development leadership begins with getting the participants and the organization focused on the outcome they want. Outcome focus avoids drama. Stephen Karpman, MD, explained drama with his drama triangle model.

In all dramas:

There is a **victim** — someone who is stuck and thinks they are being taken advantage of.

Each victim looks for a **rescuer** — someone to save them. Rescuers need to be needed. They love to find victims to "help" as it feeds their ego.

Each victim looks for a **persecutor** — someone to blame for his or her situation.

By focusing on the outcome, we know where we are going.

As the process begins, the group must leave the "old" and move toward the "new."

To get where you want to go, you must first know the general destination.

2. The Transition Curve must be recognized and managed. Moving from the status quo causes life to change. Managing this process leads to a more successful implementation.

3. Start Left of Hello — Sales are lost before hello is said. Until the fear of self-promotion and the anxiety of talking to prospective clients are overcome, there will not be a sufficient number of prospects.

4. From Hello to Infinity and Beyond — This part of the process begins at hello and continues until the prospect becomes a client.

Drumlines are fascinating with their precision and timing. The next three steps have the cadence of a drumline. Precision and timing.

Imagine the buzz around the office when success starts building. There will be excitement. Spirits will be lifted. There will be results.

It's fun when your team is meeting their prospecting goals. Having conversations with prospects, and following up with the precision and timing of a drumline.

5. The Prospecting Cadence — Pouring enough into the top of the funnel to get results.

- Identify the ideal prospect.
- How to segment your clients into strategic categories.
- How to stay on message with the prospect.
- A CRM selection process to manage the flow of information.
- How to keep tracking data from becoming the focus.
- What to do when voicemails go unanswered.
- How to separate yourself from the rest of the competition.

6. The Engagement Cadence — Talking with prospects and clients. [2]

- How to have a successful conversation.
- Four levels of questions that lead to results.
- A pre-call system to keep the conversation on track.
- Recognition of different types of needs.
- Two outcomes of every call: win or lose.
- The failure at gaining business (and it's not in closing).
- The importance of proof.
- What every prospect wants.
- Avoid the information dodge.
- Gatekeeper etiquette.
- It's never about the price.
- How to build value.
- Learn the prospect's language.

7. The Follow-up Cadence — What to do when the process continues:

- When the follow-up appointment must be made.
- Getting feedback determines the next step.

- Be a welcome guest, not an annoying pest.
- The appropriate number of times to follow up.
- How long does it take to get to "yes"?
- Voicemail jail … does anyone answer their phone?
- Talk, text, email, voicemail, cell phone processes.
- Sending emails that get answered.
- What to say after you have said it all.
- Systematize the follow-up cadence.

Fortune is found in the follow up. Given the length of the time it takes to go from the initial contact to contract follow-up is crucial. Having a cadence and follow-up reminders set in your CRM system will produce results.

There were two hippies …

Sounds like the beginning of a bad joke. It isn't. There really were two hippies in Austin, Texas, about 40 years ago. They opened a small health food store and called it "SaferWay," a play on the Safeway chain of supermarkets. They were evicted from their apartment for storing food inventory in it. They moved into their store. The store had no shower stall. They bathed using the water hose attached to their dishwasher.

Fast forward 40 years. SaferWay morphed into Whole Foods. It sold to Amazon for $13.7 billion.

Whole Foods had the right people, right plan and the right process.

For the entire story, go to the Whole Foods website.

The rest of this story is intentionally vague and unfortunately true. Here's the other side of the coin. Lack of the three Ps can end in a bad place.

During the same 40-year period there was another health food store. Unfortunately for the owner, it went out of business. The quote in the newspaper story I read was of the business owner saying, "Lately, it's been crickets. And it's kind of like we need to get out now, gracefully, while we are an awesome store instead of some little … I couldn't do it any other way."

She went on to say, "I honestly don't know what I'm going to do; I've done this my whole life. And it just breaks my heart because I was going to do this until I retired. I don't know. I think God has something else in mind for me, I don't know what it is yet. I wish I did, but I don't."

To invest 40 years into a business and have it all go away when life changes is tragic.

The Charlie Challenge is to commit to:
- The e.m.b.r.A.C.e. components of Business Development.
- Put the 7-Layer process in place.

Take into consideration the importance of the three Ps or a fourth P will show up: problems.

10. THE CIRCLE OF COMPETENCE

"I'm no genius. I'm smart in spots —
and I stay around those spots."
— Tom Watson, Sr. Founder of IBM

T he oracle of Omaha, Warren Buffett, is credited with the model "The Circle of Competence." Buffett and his partner Charlie Munger are competent investors. Their advice, that is simplified here, is worth paying attention to as you contemplate moving forward with the business development initiative.

Buffett and Munger invest in sectors that "they know they know." In looking at their company, Berkshire Hathaway, the majority of their portfolio consists of Apple, Bank of America, American Express, Coca Cola and Heinz Kraft. Those companies are in sectors they know they know.

The area outside the circle of competence is the area "they 'think' they know." Buffett and Munger avoid this area. They don't take that risk. Is it possible to make better returns outside the circle of competence? Maybe. Is it possible to be successful outside the circle of competence? Maybe. Maybe and speculation are risky.

The circle of competence is low-risk. Low-risk is safe.

Working in areas where we "think" we know is dangerous. Getting outside your circle of competence is dangerous territory. It's the thin ice. Don't let the ego eat the brain.

I've seen it happen. It's not pretty.

Chances are when someone rises up in an organization it's because, in addition to their technical skills, they have "some" people skills. That is their circle of competence.

"Technical skills and some people skills" do not necessarily equip a person to initiate and lead a business development initiative.

Rainmakers who produce results have different skills than the skills required to develop, lead, direct and sustain a business development initiative.

Marty Stuart is a well-known bluegrass musician and at one time was Johnny Cash's guitar player. Mr. Stuart made a comment in an interview that stuck with me. He said, "When someone shows up in your life, be brave enough to let them in."

Fear shuts out opportunity. We can attribute the loss of opportunity to the amygdala in our brain. It is the "dinosaur brain," focused on "survival." The amygdala spends its time looking for problems. Some people have well-developed skills at shutting out opportunities. Consider the benefits of being open-minded enough to consider the benefit of staying in your circle of competence.

We never enjoy the benefit of what we don't have. Saying no to just considering an opportunity is the amygdala in action. Consider the benefits.

I'm about six feet tall. I presented a client with an idea and as I explained the opportunity, I spread my arms out wide open to demonstrate being open to possibilities and opportunity. One of the partners commented it would be a good reminder to put that pose on the wall as a reminder to look at opportunity from all angles, with eyes wide open. And to consider the benefits.

If you are wavering back and forth and being indecisive about moving forward with improving your business development results, let's look inside the brain and see why that happens. Our brain gets stuck in survival mode. We get trapped by our own thoughts.

A short reminder course about how the three parts of the brain functions is:

- The dinosaur part of the brain is the part that helps us survive. This helps us breathe in and out without thinking about it. This part helps us survive as it triggers the fight-or-flight response.
- The next layer of the brain is the limbic part. This part helps us make decisions, such as what we want for lunch.
- The most evolved part of the brain is the neocortex. It helps us with problem-solving and reasoning.

The dinosaur part of the brain, the survival part, won't help solve problems and think through decisions. When it's strategic decision time and we notice we are being indecisive or struggling, we are using the survival or the dinosaur part of our brain. We are protecting ourselves and surviving.

It's time for a brain shift.

To shift out of survival mode and into the problem-solving and reasoning functions found in the neocortex, we need to shift our thinking to reframe our thoughts.

An example of when this shift occurs is when we are in the shower. The water is hitting us, we are shampooing our hair, our focus changes and shifts. Our thoughts shift to the neocortex and "bam," a new thought or a great idea comes to us.

We had a brain shift.

I understand you can't jump in the shower at the office to shift your thinking. How do we implement a shift in our thinking?

Another tip from David Emerald's work around transforming drama into productivity tells us to look up from this book and look around the room. Find five red things. As we shift our focus from the book and begin searching, we have a brain shift. We shift from survival to problem-solving.

The shift works and helps us get unstuck. Do the exercise to get unstuck by finding five red things and you'll notice a difference in your thinking.

There are three options available to you to grow your practice and improve business development results.

Option 1. You can stick with the status quo and do nothing. You know how that is working. And ... continue buying the excuses of your staff and prospects and yourself as to why it's OK to settle for less than what you wanted out of your career or your business.

Option 2. You can read this book, implement the solutions yourself and take a risk by hiring someone to help improve your business development results. Hiring someone using the subjective interview model you used in the past is a risk. (See Chapter 3 about hiring problems and unknowingly teaching your people their bad habits).

Option 3. Get Charlie Moon. I have 40 years experience developing business development programs. The past 30 of those years are in the professional services niche.

Before working together, we will dig in together to understand:

- Where you are in your business development program.
- Where you want to take your business.
- How we are going to get there.
- What will happen along the way.

The work I do comes with a 100% guarantee.

There's no risk to you. If at any point when we are working together you believe you are not receiving the value you are investing in your business development program, we stop working together.

It's that simple. I believe in the engineered process I deliver. It works. I am willing to accept the risk based on the objectives we agree on before we begin.

Two points to consider when hiring someone as an employee

Consideration 1. When you hire an employee, you really don't know what you are getting until the commitment is made. Hiring someone else's problem is a problem.

Behavioral assessments quantify behavior. In the stories people tell us about themselves while answering the profile questions, we are able to assess what we're getting and predict if their bad twin brother will show up.

Again, there are two kinds of hiring managers: 1. those who admit to making hiring mistakes, and 2. those in denial.

If you hire enough people, at some point you will hire a mistake if you use a subjective process of asking and answering questions and checking references. And on references, seriously, anyone can find three people to say good things about them.

In today's world, you can Google "how to interview" and read what the authors say about what questions to ask. The candidate can Google "how to be interviewed" and read what the authors say about how to answer the questions that are asked. The subjective process is risky. The objective process is … well … objective.

Consideration 2. Hiring an employee is like buying the kids a pony. The pony will need to be fed every day. Every day. Every day. When the kids get bored with the pony, the pony still gets fed. The pony gets fed every day whether the kids ride the pony or not.

If you take a risk and hire someone using a subjective process, the person you hire will eat every day. If you take a risk and hire someone else's problem, it is expensive.

These risks are real and they eat every day. They eat payroll dollars. They eat producers. They eat prospects. They eat margin. Hiring a mistake is expensive. Don't do it.

Staying in the circle of competence contributes to you operating where "you know you know." It is not a sign of weakness to ask for help, although I recognize that is difficult for some people to do. Some of you will believe you need to "just figure it out."

You don't need to figure it out, because living outside the circle of competence is dangerously thin ice.

11. TOP 11 BIGGEST MISTAKES

---

1. Working harder

It doesn't matter if you are a solopreneur or a managing partner of a large firm. Simply working harder is similar to climbing to the top of a ladder to learn it has been leaned against the wrong wall.

Bringing in a fresh perspective with a different set of lenses in their glasses lets new thoughts, ideas and processes permeate the culture. This stops complacency with long-term staff members and sets the expectation with less tenured staff.

2. Being too proud to ask for help

None of us knows it all. We live with those nagging doubts that keep us from getting the help we want. Some people are OK with asking for help. Some people are not. Be one who asks.

3. Piecemealing the process

Cutting corners is expensive and risky. Partial implementation of the process creates a fourth P — problems.

Calculate the cost of recruiting, interviewing, and selecting staff members. Add on the investment made to train them, pay them while they familiarize themselves with your products and services, and then multiply what it costs to have them miss opportunities and fail.

Being "pretty good" or "OK" at business development is expensive and risky. Be excellent.

Making decisions based on misdirected speculation and opinions rather than quantified results based on experience and knowledge creates a gap in results. That gap is high-risk with no reward.

Do not piecemeal this initiative. Do not present "hello to thank you" training in a vacuum. That's a waste of time and money. Bringing in a motivational speaker a few times a year will produce sporadic results for a short time. Hiring local training talent that "also does some sales training" is not a sustainable process for long-term development.

4. Ignoring the validity of visibility management

Relying on the technical skills of your profession results in career stagnation. At some point, something needs to be sold. Everyone sells.

5. Using the wrong process

When the sales process doesn't match the product and service, the results are dismal and expensive.

When bits and pieces of the e.m.b.r.A.C.e. model are chosen, there will be a gap in learning and results. A lack of accountability and consistency will result in subpar results.

6. Forgetting that people are people

When transition occurs and life changes, it can get messy. People struggling to maintain a sense of dignity and respect need empathy and leadership.

They need to be appreciated as a person. They have kids and dogs and soccer practice. They want a leader who will direct, coach, and support them as they transition from order taker to rainmaker.

7. Operating outside the circle of competence

Letting the ego eat the brain is high-risk with low probability for success.
Get the help and coaching you need to assist you in making this transition from "what is" to "what will be."

8. When help shows up, not letting them in

It's a mistake to be guided by fear. Delaying a decision until it is perfect, is another mistake. Fear of failure leads to failure.

9. Getting pulled into the drama

When life changes and people begin to traverse the transition zone, it can be treacherous. Be on the lookout for the drama triangle. Focus on the outcome.

10. Not saying hello

The most important word is "hello." We may not know what will happen when we say hello, but I guarantee nothing happens until we do.

People are people. Acknowledge them. Say hello when they come in for the day. Acknowledge them when they leave at night.

Let people see you are a person. Be vulnerable. Admit when you have made a mistake. Acknowledge when you have struggled. This admission encourages them.

11. Thinking problems solve themselves

Problems don't solve themselves. They get worse.
As it was in the beginning of this book, there are still two kinds of people: the kind who like to talk about their problems and the kind who like to solve their problems.

Your visibility management problem hasn't gone away while you've read this book. It may have gotten worse.

12. FOCUS FORWARD

"If I don't build it, I'll never know."
— *Bob Moon*

My brother Bob had a heart transplant at 56. He was an architect and real estate development guy. Bob enjoyed life, people, woodworking, and building mobiles. Not long after his heart transplant, Bob called me on the phone. He told me he was going to build a studio addition on their house.

It would be a studio large enough for his books, computer, woodworking tools and metalworking equipment. Bob was excited to have a project to design and build.

When I asked, "Bob what are you going to do in your studio"? Bob's optimistic outlook came through loud and clear when he said, "I don't know, but if I don't build it, I'll never know."

Be like Bob.

Be like Bob about your foray into business development.

Make your mantras:
- If I don't say hello to a prospect, I'll never know if they'll become a client.
- If I don't develop a conversation cadence and follow the process, I'll never know if the process works.
- If I don't develop a follow-up cadence and follow the process,

I'll never know the opportunities that were missed.

We can't:
- Change the past.
- Rely on technical skills to grow a business.
- Doubt the importance of visibility.
- Doubt the significance of the importance of business development.
- Wing it on prospect and client calls.
- Aggressively wait for the phone to ring.

We can:
- Stop the excuses.
- Grow the practice.
- Stop being invisible.
- Gain clarity on business development.
- Overcome fears.
- Comfortably talk to strangers.
- Find a process that works.
- Not be too proud to get help.

As it is with all things, the best place to start is where you are.

For a closer look at current reality with no cost to you, go to getcharliemoon.com Complete the business development checkup. Schedule a strategy call.

Email me at charlie@getcharliemoon.com and schedule a call to answer your questions. During our conversation, we'll see if we are a fit to work together.

I learned in 4th grade, when I won my first sales contest, that the most important word to say is "hello." Let's say hello and have a conversation about where you are, and where you want to go.

I Googled it. There are no search results for "number of people who die after saying hello." It won't happen. Say hello.

Aaron Baker, a bank senior vice president had this to say about me and the process I developed:

> *"Charlie Moon asks the questions you need to answer about where you've been, where you are, and where you want to go. He walks with you, as you confront the obstacles between yourself and your goals. The conversations can be difficult, and the answers hard to face. However, Charlie has been through the fire and will show you the way to the other side. The way to success. He will be with you through the journey, and you'll be better off for the experience."*

There is no try ...

At this point, it may be tempting to say, "We'll try to do better." The harsh truth about trying is you can't. You can't try. You can't try to hand someone a glass of water. Either the glass of water is handed over or it's not handed over.

There is "do" and there is "don't do." There is no try. When someone says "try," it's just a noisy way of not doing something. Try to turn the page of this book.

Since you're still reading, you've demonstrated you can't try. You either turned the page or you didn't. There is no try.

Get committed for your commitment to your commitment

Bill Koch, a self-proclaimed hick from Kansas (whose net worth hovers around $1.8 billion) won the America's Cup in 1992. His friends told him he should "get committed for his commitment to his commitment."

When you make the commitment to move your business development program forward, stay committed to your commitment. Then, the only thing left to do is to do it.

It may be tempting to settle for "good enough." Your empathetic heart may be tempted to allow self-limiting beliefs and behavior to control you or your people. Don't let off the gas, and lose focus. Please. You have invested time and energy and money into this initiative. Getting distracted and losing your way keeps you from enjoying the benefits that come from developing your staff.

A partial list of benefits of staying the course and focusing forward include:
- An increase in revenue.
- Your status increases amongst your peers.
- Respect from competitors that observe your staff in action.
- Camaraderie increases as the team develops.
- Tension decreases as results increase.
- Staff members grow and gain confidence.
- You'll stop feeling defeated about business development.

Remember, there are two kinds of people: the kind who like to talk about their problems and the kind who like to solve their problems.

Problems don't solve themselves. They get worse.

Initiatives have two components: content and process. The results-oriented business development process outlined in this book draws on the models and processes I use when I work with clients in the professional services niche.

The process remains the same. Trust the process. This process starts before hello is said. After we have addressed and corrected the emotional short-circuit that occurs when it's time to prospect, we continue on the journey from hello to infinity and beyond.

With the length of the major account sales process, it may seem like it will take to infinity and beyond to convert a prospect to a client. Content is the story that is told to prospects. Content changes. Process remains the same.

If, (and I've always thought "if" should be an 11 syllable word, because IF is a big word) … if you follow the process that is in this book, you will meet with some success. I encourage you to not piecemeal this initiative. Don't present "hello to thank you" training in a vacuum. That's a waste of time and money.

Bringing in a motivational speaker a few times a year will produce sporadic results for a short time. Hiring local training talent that "also does some sales training" is not a sustainable process; it's a waste of money.

Google The Ebbinghaus Forgetting Curve, click on "images" and you'll see how quickly what is heard in a "hit it and quit it" one-time presentation is forgotten. Twenty minutes after the material is covered, 42% of the material is forgotten. After 31 days, 79% of the material presented is forgotten. Retention occurs through repetition and use.

Learn. Do. Learn. Do. Repeat. That is a mantra that works.

There are going to be days when participants don't want to call one more prospect. That's the very reason to make one more call. Your role as the leader is to pay it forward. It's time to be an encourager to those who are struggling.

Look for the good in what they are doing

At some point, we have all had someone help and support us. Perry Wiggins, my 8th grade English teacher, helped me prepare for my first speech contest. Bill Heilmann, my college advisor, helped me develop my stage presence.

Neither Wiggins nor Heilmann could see far enough ahead to know that in my career I would develop and deliver over 2,000 workshops. I appreciate the investment they made in me.

Your people will appreciate the investment you make in them. Your hard work has gotten you where you are in your career. Now it's time to pay it forward and invest in those around you.

Through it all, enjoy the ride. Enjoy the opportunity to repay the opportunity you were given.

Focus Forward tactics that work include:

- Encouragement works.
- Encourage in public.
- Correct in private.
- Find the good.
- Be about improvement, not competition.
- Be about improvement, not comparison.
- Build trust.
- Keep commitments.
- Provide proof.
- Develop process.

No one is "over-appreciated" at work. People like to feel appreciated beyond a paycheck.

Be 100% committed to do the work to make this work. Commit for you, your organization and your people.

Focus on the outcome ... and then ... focus forward.

As you focus forward and move forward you'll see:

- Progress begins.
- Synergy happens.
- Confidence gained.
- Order takers become rainmakers.
- People
  - Let go of the past.
  - Not take exit ramps.
  - Survive and thrive.

- The light goes on about the importance of visibility.
- Skeptics and nonbelievers become believers.
- Curious onlookers wanting to participate.
- Normal people become successful.
- A stop to the excuses.

I have seen these bullet points happen. There are more.

It's likely you could list people who would benefit if/when this process is implemented at your organization. There are processes you've read about here that would work well in your company.

Make a list to be able to refer back on good ideas you've seen here. Make a list.

I'll wait.

Benefits I see from implementing what I've read in this book:

When I work with an organization, it is written into the letter of engagement that the work I do is guaranteed to work.

If, at any point, a client decides he or she is not receiving the value of their investment, we stop. It works for all of us. There is no risk.

There are people who try to make "the perfect decision." That's part of the "out-perfect" we talked about earlier, where the fear of failure causes people to fail. Don't wrestle with making the perfect decision. Make the decision you make perfect. Work to make it perfect.

It is time to decide. You can decide to put the book on the bookshelf and continue to do the same things, expecting different results.

Or you can decide to build your business.

What will happen?

If you don't build it, you'll never know.

One thing for sure is if you don't build it, it could well be your worst hell.

NEXT STEPS

At this point, there are some options available to help. The options range from:

1. Do nothing. Maintain the status quo. Risk failure.

2. Complete the Business Development Checkup by going to getcharliemoon.com and scheduling a strategy call.

3. Contact me with specific questions ranging from visibility management, where we start "before hello" all the way through "to infinity and beyond."

> *Email me at charlie@getcharliemoon.com. I'll send you some free helpful resources.*

Please contact me when you have further questions or need some clarification on a topic.

Nothing happens until we say hello.

HERE'S WHAT THEY'RE SAYING ABOUT CHARLIE MOON

"I learned the value of visibility"

"Charlie made it fun"

"Great speaker, really learned something"

"Most important, Charlie is honest"

"The assessment he uses identified why I felt as if I were spinning in circles."

"My company and personal sales have increased tremendously."
—Juvetta Slane

"He (Charlie) is a great storyteller and uses his understanding of human nature to draw participants into the subject and encourage their growth. A consummate professional and a joy to work with."
— April Scott | Mid-America All-Indian Center

"Charlie has been ideal to work with. He is responsive, prepared and dependable. Fully engages the audience. Exceptional at answering questions, providing factual and helpful information. Charlie's in-

nate friendliness, curiosity and interest in others creates an almost immediate bond with the audience. His regular injection of joviality and humor keeps the attention and engagement of the audience."
— *Alicia Holloway | Wichita Independent Business Association*

"The most observant person I have ever met."
— *Lyman Bowling | Media entrepreneur*

"Very insightful. I especially liked what he had to say about closing the deal and introduction to strangers."
— *Anonymous participant evaluation*

"Charlie was great. He knew his stuff and made you feel comfortable. He kept things light yet pointed out everything, presenting it in a professional manner."
— *Anonymous participant evaluation*

"When we hired Charlie Moon to help us with our sales efforts at KTLI Light 99 FM, we were a new radio station in the market with a young and underdeveloped sales staff. Charlie helped us hire qualified sellers, train, retain and develop them to be effective, and make a difference for the businesses they contacted in our market.

"Charlie focused our sellers on finding the client's needs and meeting them with creative solutions. He also worked to diminish their call reluctance and turn our sellers into a marketing resource for each of their clients.

"Charlie made a dramatic impact on the results achieved by our sales team. The increases were significant. I'd highly recommend that you get Charlie Moon for your team."
— *John Pohlman, Rainmaker*

The book you hold in your hand is the business development shortcut you've been looking for. Most firms lose the deal before they ever say "hello."

Inside you'll discover the 7-Layer Business Development Process that has turned smart, but sales-averse, accountants, bankers, architects, and buttoned-down professionals of every stripe into willing and consistently successful rainmakers. It will do the same for you and the professionals in your firm.

If your firm "aggressively waits for the phone to ring," as one managing partner once told me, then you need this book. It will put you back in control of your business development, once and for all.

Nothing happens until we say, "Hello,"

CHARLIE MOON

Made in the USA
Coppell, TX
20 July 2021

59198735R30056